D1265605

CARTOON·NATION presents
EST. 1776
POLITICAL ELECTIONS

by Davis Worth Miller and
Katherine McLean Brevard
illustrated by Charles Barnett III

CONSULTANT:
Michael Bailey
Colonel William J. Walsh Associate Professor
of American Government
Georgetown University, Washington, D.C.

Capstone
press

Mankato, Minnesota

Graphic Library is published by Capstone Press,
151 Good Counsel Drive, P.O. Box 669, Mankato, Minnesota 56002.
www.capstonepress.com

1 2 3 4 5 6 13 12 11 10 09 08

Library of Congress Cataloging-in-Publication Data
Miller, Davis Worth.
    Political elections / by Davis Worth Miller and Katherine McLean Brevard; illustrated
by Charles Barnett III.
    p. cm. — (Graphic Library. Cartoon nation)
    Summary: "In cartoon format, explains the history of voting rights and the function of
political elections in the United States" — Provided by publisher.
    Includes bibliographical references and index.
    ISBN-13: 978-1-4296-1333-0 (hardcover)
    ISBN-10: 1-4296-1333-5 (hardcover)
    ISBN-13: 978-1-4296-1780-2 (softcover pbk.)
    ISBN-10: 1-4296-1780-2 (softcover pbk.)
    1. Elections — United States — Juvenile literature. 2. Voting — United States —
Juvenile literature. I. Miller, Davis Worth II. Brevard, Katherine McLean. III. Barnett,
Charles, IV, ill. V. Title. VI. Series.
JK1978.M55 2008
324.973 — dc22   2007031041

Art Direction and Design
Bob Lentz

Cover Artist
Kelly Brown

Colorist
Michael Kelleher

Editor
Christine Peterson

Editor's note: Direct quotations from primary sources are indicated by a yellow background.

Direct quotations appear on the following pages:
Page 11 (top left), from the *Status of Women: Past, Present, and Future* by Susan B. Anthony
    (1897, publisher unknown).
Page 11 (top center), from a 1911 speech by Carrie Chapman Catt as recorded in
    Feminism: The Essential Historical Writings, edited by Miriam Schneir (New York:
    Vintage Books, 1994).
Page 11 (top right), from a speech by Elizabeth Cady Stanton, as recorded in *The Elizabeth
    Cady Stanton–Susan B. Anthony Reader: Correspondence, Writings, Speeches*, edited by
    Ellen Carol DuBois (Boston: Northeastern University Press, 1981).
Page 26 (top left) oath of office for U.S. president, as stated in the U.S. Constitution
    (http://www.archives.gov/national-archives-experience/charters/constitution_transcript
    html).
Page 26 (top right), oath of office for members of the U.S. Congress (http://www.senate.gov).

TABLE OF CONTENTS

EST. CARTOON NATION 1776

19.00 M J

4-1-08 Capstone

264 6971

Every four years, citizens of the United States take part in the country's largest election.

Who got your vote for president?

I'm not going to tell you that, dear. Voting is a private matter.

But voting for president is just one part of the U.S. election process. Citizens also elect other leaders including county sheriffs, court judges, and state governors.

I am proud to be the governator — I mean governor — of the great state of California.

ARNOLD SCHWARZENEGGER

And elections aren't just for adults. Kids get to vote for leaders in their schools and other organizations.

In fact, elections are so common many people take them for granted. But not everyone has always had the right to vote and run for office. When this country began, people had very few rights at all.

BALLOT BASICS

The origin of the English word ballot is the Italian word *ballotta*, which means "a colored ball." In 13th century Italy, people used small balls to cast their votes.

In the 1600s, America was a group of 13 colonies controlled by Great Britain. The British government imposed laws and taxes upon the colonies. Colonists did not have a say in the British government.

Colonists strongly believed that people should be represented in their government. Each colony held elections for local laws and leaders. But colonies also limited voting rights to white men who owned land or paid a certain amount in taxes.

But by the late 1700s, changes were brewing for the colonies and elections. Britain's King George forced colonists to pay heavy taxes on common goods like paper and tea.

The king's taxes make my blood boil!

In 1775, American colonists went to war against Great Britain. In 1783, colonists won their independence. After the war, U.S. leaders formed a new democratic government. Leaders tried to balance power between national and state governments.

GEORGE WASHINGTON

BENJAMIN FRANKLIN

Whoa, Ben, that's a lot of state power you're putting in. Be careful, this thing could blow up!

With every great experiment, my dear George, there are great risks.

In 1788, states approved a new Constitution that mapped out basic rights and laws for the nation.

All these new laws, and still only white men who own land can vote.

COUNTING KERNELS

One of the earliest ways to vote in colonial America used beans and corn kernels to count votes. Another method was the voice vote. Voters shouted a name or yelled "aye" or "nay" to vote for someone.

Oh, no! There goes another vote for Isaac!

In the 1800s, the United States continued to grow and more states joined the Union. Voting laws also changed to meet the needs of a growing nation. In most states, all white men were allowed to vote, whether or not they owned property.

Yippee-kaiyo-kaiyay! I finally got to vote!

Looks like they forgot about us again.

But new voting rules did not include African Americans and women. Most African Americans in the southern United States were slaves. They had no rights and were not allowed to vote. Far worse, slaves were considered property.

By 1860, the issue of slavery divided the nation. A civil war broke out between northern and southern states. The North won the Civil War in 1865. Soon, the country passed the 13th Amendment ending slavery in the United States. In 1870, the 15th Amendment to the Constitution extended voting rights to African American men.

Great teamwork, guys. I'm glad you're here.

Despite changes to the Constitution, African American men were still denied the right to vote. Black men had to pass a test or pay a fee before they were allowed to vote. Some white officials hid or changed the location of polling places to prevent African American men from voting. Worse yet, some people threatened and even killed African American men who tried to vote.

In the 1960s, a **civil rights** movement forced changes in voting rights. In 1964, the U.S. government passed the Civil Rights Act ending discrimination in public places or on the job.

Keep pushing! We're almost there.

civil rights — the rights that all people have to freedom and equal treatment under the law

The Voting Rights Act of 1965 banned tests at polling places. This law also allowed the government to take action against voting practices that discriminated against voters.

Although African American men had won the right to vote in 1870, U.S. women had not. In most states, women of all races still could not vote in elections or hold elected office. In the mid-1800s, thousands of women protested in favor of voting rights.

Women deserve the right to vote . . .

For the next 50 years, women held hundreds of protests, rallies, and speeches in support of voting rights. Thousands of women were arrested for wanting the same rights as men.

Are you paying attention to any of this?

I can be arrested, but I still can't vote.

In 1920, the 19th Amendment to the Constitution became law. Women now had the right to vote and hold political office in the United States. Voting rights were advanced thanks to the work of many women, including Susan B. Anthony, Carrie Chapman Catt, and Elizabeth Cady Stanton.

SUSAN B. ANTHONY

CARRIE CHAPMAN CATT

ELIZABETH CADY STANTON

There never will be complete equality until women themselves help to make laws and elect lawmakers.

In the adjustment of the new order of things, we women demand an equal voice; we shall accept nothing less.

The right is ours. Have it we must. Use it we will!

Although it was a long struggle, the United States wasn't the last country to allow women to vote. Women in France and Italy won voting rights in the 1940s. In Switzerland, women weren't allowed to vote until 1971.

This door had better open soon or we'll have to break it down.

VOTING RIGHTS

We western women have the voting spirit!

JEANNETTE RANKIN

RANKIN RULES

In 1917, Jeannette Rankin of Montana became the first woman elected to the U.S. House of Representatives. At that time, Montana was one of the few U.S. states where women were allowed to vote.

11

In the United States, most citizens over age 18 can vote in elections. Many people feel so strongly about taking part in government that they join political parties. Political parties are groups of people who share similar ideas about how the country should be run.

Members of political parties build a platform of ideas about how they believe the country should be managed. And they choose **candidates** to run for political office.

candidate — a person who runs for elected office

The United States has two main political parties. The donkey is the Democratic Party's symbol. Democrats believe the donkey shows that the party is strong and dependable. The Republican symbol is the elephant. Republicans say this symbol shows their party's strength and intelligence.

You can always count on me.

You may be dependable, but I've got the brains.

But candidates don't have to belong to the Republican or Democratic parties to run for office. Some people belong to third parties. Third-party candidates often take on issues they feel the main political parties have ignored.

We can always build on leftover issues.

ENVIRONMENT
JOBS
TAXES

CHOOSING CANDIDATES

Parties choose one candidate to run for each government office. Candidates represent the party's goals and ideas during the election.

Aww, I hate nuts.

In many elections, several members of one political party want to run for the same office. Party members do their best to weed out candidates with lesser skills than others. They want the best candidate for the job on the ballot. That way, their party has a better shot at winning an election.

ANIMAL ATTRACTION

Animals aren't allowed to vote. But, goofy as it sounds, they have held political office. A recent mayor of Rabbit Hash, Kentucky, was Junior Cochran, a black Labrador retriever. Mayor Clay Henry III of Lajitas, Texas, was a goat. And Paco Bell, a donkey, was recently elected to his second term as mayor of Florissant, Colorado.

To choose the best candidate for the election, political parties often hold a run-off or **primary election**. Primaries feature political party front-runners and candidates who are favored by special interest groups.

Candidates in these races don't actually have to run anywhere. In primary elections, voters choose the candidate to best represent their party in an election. The party candidate with the most votes wins a spot on the final ballot.

Party members also gather every four years for national conventions. These gatherings include speeches, cheering, and loud music.

primary election — an election in which voters choose the party candidates who will run for office

But conventions aren't all fun and games. Party members choose a candidate to run for U.S. president.

Each candidate must follow certain rules for the elected office. And if you want to become president, you have to follow rules presented in the Constitution.

The President of the United States must be at least 35 years old . . .

I'm that.

Rats, I'm only 11.

ARNOLD SCHWARZENEGGER

Presidents must have lived in the United States for at least the past 14 years . . .

I've done that.

I'm getting close.

Presidents must have been born in the United States.

Ah, shucks. I was born in Austria.

Too bad for you, governor. I was born in Toledo!

OFFICE RULES

Other national offices have requirements as well. U.S. senators must be at least 30 years old. They must be U.S. citizens who have lived in the country at least nine years. A U.S. representative must be 25 years old and a citizen who's lived here at least seven years.

Candidates for political office combine many talents. Candidates are usually good speakers and strong leaders. And the more experience they have in politics, the better.

But experience in government isn't always needed if the candidate is famous. Famous people get elected to political office because they are well-known to voters.

GOVERNOR
JESSE VENTURA

MAYOR
CLINT
EASTWOOD

GOVERNOR
ARNOLD
SCHWARZENEGGER

War heroes have also been elected to many public offices, including U.S. president. Dwight D. Eisenhower was a popular World War II hero. In 1952, both the Republican and Democratic parties wanted him as their presidential nominee.

We like Ike.

DWIGHT D. EISENHOWER

Yeah, well we like him more!

CRAZY CAMPAIGNS

In the late 1700s and early 1800s, political campaigns were quiet affairs. Most candidates thought it was bad manners to campaign for votes.

Campaigns changed in 1828 when John Quincy Adams and Andrew Jackson squared off for the presidency. Jackson toured the nation and gave many public speeches, often standing on tree stumps so the crowds could see him.

stump — to make political speeches during a campaign for elected office

In the late 1800s, railroads roared across the country and candidates were quick to hop on board. Trains allowed candidates to cover more ground than ever before, giving speeches and talking with people.

We're riding the rails to victory!

By the 1920s, candidates used radio to get their messages out to voters. In the 1950s, debates on TV allowed millions of people to hear candidates' opinions. Today, candidates pop up on radio, TV, and the Internet.

And despite technology, you'll still see candidates walking in parades, handing out fliers, and meeting voters.

Travel, TV appearances, and fancy dinners sound like fun, right? But campaigns are also a lot of hard work. Candidates from opposing parties compete for the public's attention and votes.

And voters can be very picky. During a campaign, voters and the news media keep a close eye on candidates. If a candidates sneezes, the public's going to hear about it. Candidates must answer questions about both political issues and their private lives.

I hope they don't look too close.

For candidates, campaigns are long and expensive journeys. Campaign costs add up fast. How do candidates raise all this money? Well, it doesn't grow on trees.

Candidates receive donations from average citizens, celebrities, and business leaders. Candidates promise to work on issues important to these groups.

But campaign funding has its limits. Laws limit how much money people or groups can donate to a campaign. And many voters question whether donations make for a fair campaign. Many voters worry that **politicians** will do what donors want, instead of what's best for the people.

politician —
someone who
runs for or holds
political office

GOVERNMENT FOR THE PEOPLE

When a majority of citizens vote, the government takes notice. Elected officials have a clear idea of what citizens expect from their government.

It's the public, Mr. President. They want to speak with you.

I've been expecting their call.

People who move to the United States can become citizens and gain the right to vote. In the United States, millions of people have studied hard and passed a citizenship test to earn the right to vote.

IMMIGRATION OFFICE

MEET MAYOR MIKE

Some young adults show their interest in government not only by voting, but also by running for office. In 2004, 18-year-old high school student Michael Sessions was elected mayor of Hillsdale, Michigan, a town of about 8,200 people. Michael's campaign cost only $700 and was paid for with money he saved from his summer job selling toffee apples.

But what if you're out of the country on Election Day? No problem. Citizens can still vote. They just need to send in their ballot before Election Day. Millions of people now cast absentee ballots. Even astronauts.

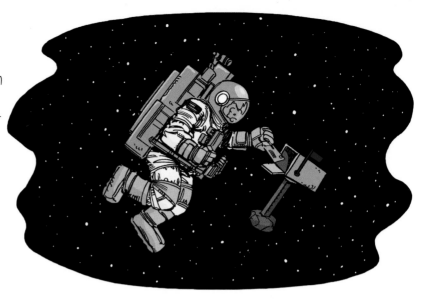

Even with all this opportunity, more Americans choose not to vote than people in other democratic countries.

Since 1845, elections have been held on the first Tuesday following the first Monday in November. Back then most Americans were farmers. Once harvest was completed, they had more time to vote.

Sir, you can no longer vote with corn. We use paper ballots now.

In the 1800s, people often traveled 100 miles to vote. Today, most polling places are close to voters' homes.

Ballots! Get your ballots here.

Ballots are different from state to state and town to town. Some voters use paper ballots or punch cards. Some people vote by pulling a handle on a machine. More and more people vote by computer.

Each voter may only complete one ballot. Each ballot has a long list of candidates for local, state, and national offices. Voters choose one person for each office on the ballot.

In most cases, the candidate with the most votes wins the election. But that's not the case when you're voting for U.S. president. When voting for president, citizens are actually choosing a group of electors who make up the Electoral College. Electors from each state cast the final votes for president. A candidate must receive at least 271 electoral votes to become president.

ROLLER-COASTER RACE

Elections don't always go smoothly. In fact, they can be full of suspense. Take the presidential election of 2000, for example. Democrat Al Gore and Republican George W. Bush rode a roller coaster of election results. As the votes were counted, sometimes Gore was in the lead and other times Bush was ahead. In the end, Gore won the popular vote but Bush received 271 electoral votes to become the 43rd president.

Soon after the elections are over, the winning candidates take office and get to work. And there's plenty of work waiting for them. Bills, laws, and countless messages from citizens like you greet newly elected leaders.

OATH OF OFFICE FOR U.S. PRESIDENT

I will, to the best of my ability, preserve, protect and defend the Constitution of the United States . . .

OATH OF OFFICE FOR U.S. CONGRESS

I will support and defend the Constitution of the United States against all enemies . . .

Elected leaders also learn how to balance the needs and wants of people they serve. Elected leaders must represent all citizens, not just those who voted for them. Public officials must balance their opinions and ideas with those of the citizens they represent.

ABRAHAM LINCOLN

Ladies and gentlemen, this is no trick. You're watching a government of the people, by the people, and for the people.

As citizens, it's important for us to pay attention to what our leaders do in office. Do they follow through on their promises? Do they take action on issues important to people in their city, state, or country? If not, you can help elect new leaders who will.

Even though kids can't vote, they can still make their mark on government. Today, kids are speaking out on issues facing their community and country.

In the United States, almost anyone can be elected to a public office. You could too. You could be elected to serve on the student council or other organization. As an adult, you could be elected a mayor, governor, senator, representative, or even president.

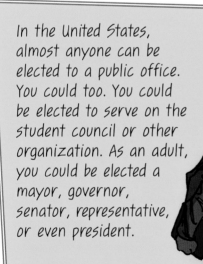

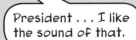

President . . . I like the sound of that.

TIME LINE

1629 — The first secret, written ballot is used in America to choose a minister for a church in Salem, Massachusetts.

1629

JUNE 21, 1788

February 3, 1870 — The 15th Amendment extends voting rights to African American men.

August 18, 1920 —The 19th Amendment to the U.S. Constitution becomes law and extends voting rights to women.

FEBRUARY 3, 1870

AUGUST 18, 1920

August 6, 1965 — President Lyndon B. Johnson signs the Voting Rights Act into law. It provides federal protection for African Americans who want to register to vote.

AUGUST 6, 1965

June 21, 1788 — U.S. states approve the Constitution. The Constitution allows states to decide who can vote. In the original 13 states, only white men who owned land and paid taxes could vote.

February 4, 1789 — George Washington is elected the first president of the United States by a group of 69 electors from 10 of the 13 states.

July 1848 — Women gather at the Seneca Falls Convention to discuss voting rights for women.

FEBRUARY 4, 1789

JULY 1848

July 1, 1971 — The 26th Amendment is approved and lowers the voting age from 21 to age 18.

YOU MUST BE 18 YEARS OLD TO VOTE.

October 29, 2002 — The Help America Vote Act is passed. It provides states with money to buy voting machines and is intended to make sure all votes are counted.

JULY 1, 1971

OCTOBER 29, 2002

GLOSSARY

amendment (uh-MEND-muhnt) — a change made to a law or a legal document

ballot (BA-luht) — a punch card, piece of paper, or electronic screen on which a person's vote is recorded

campaign (kam-PAYN) — to try to gain support from people in order to win an election

candidate (KAN-duh-dayt) — a person who runs for elected office

civil rights (SI-vil RYTS) — the rights that all people have to freedom and equal treatment under the law

political party (puh-LIT-uh-kuhl PAR-tee) — a group of people who share the same beliefs about how the government should operate

politician (pol-uh-TISH-uhn) — someone who runs for or holds government office

polling place (POHL-ing PLAYSS)—the place where people vote in an election

primary election (PRYE-mair-ee e-LEHK-shuhn) — an election in which voters choose the party candidates who will run for office

stump (STUHMP) — to make political speeches during a campaign for elected office

READ MORE

Burgan, Michael. *Political Parties*. Cartoon Nation. Mankato, Minn.: Capstone Press, 2008.

Giddens-White, Byron. *National Elections and the Political Process*. Our Government. Chicago: Heinemann, 2006.

Hamilton, John. *Voting in an Election*. Government in Action! Edina, Minn.: Abdo, 2005.

Liljeblad, Fredrik. *Voting*: Citizens and Their Governments. Ann Arbor, Mich.: Cherry Lake, 2008.

INTERNET SITES

FactHound offers a safe, fun way to find Internet sites related to this book. All of the sites on FactHound have been researched by our staff.

Here's how:
1. Visit www.facthound.com
2. Choose your grade level.
3. Type in this book ID 1429613335 for age-appropriate sites. You may also browse subjects by clicking on letters, or by clicking on pictures and words.
4. Click on the Fetch It button.

FactHound will fetch the best sites for you!

INDEX